WORLD LANDMARKS

LEVEL **3** READER
GRADES 2 TO 4 — READING LEVEL

Written by Kathryn Knight

bendon®

Colosseum

Rome, Italy

This old, old theater was built by the Romans between 70–80 A.D.—almost 2,000 years ago. It could hold 50,000 people! They watched gladiator fights, animal shows, and plays. And the entire bottom level could be flooded to hold boats for mock sea battles!

...and some are new.

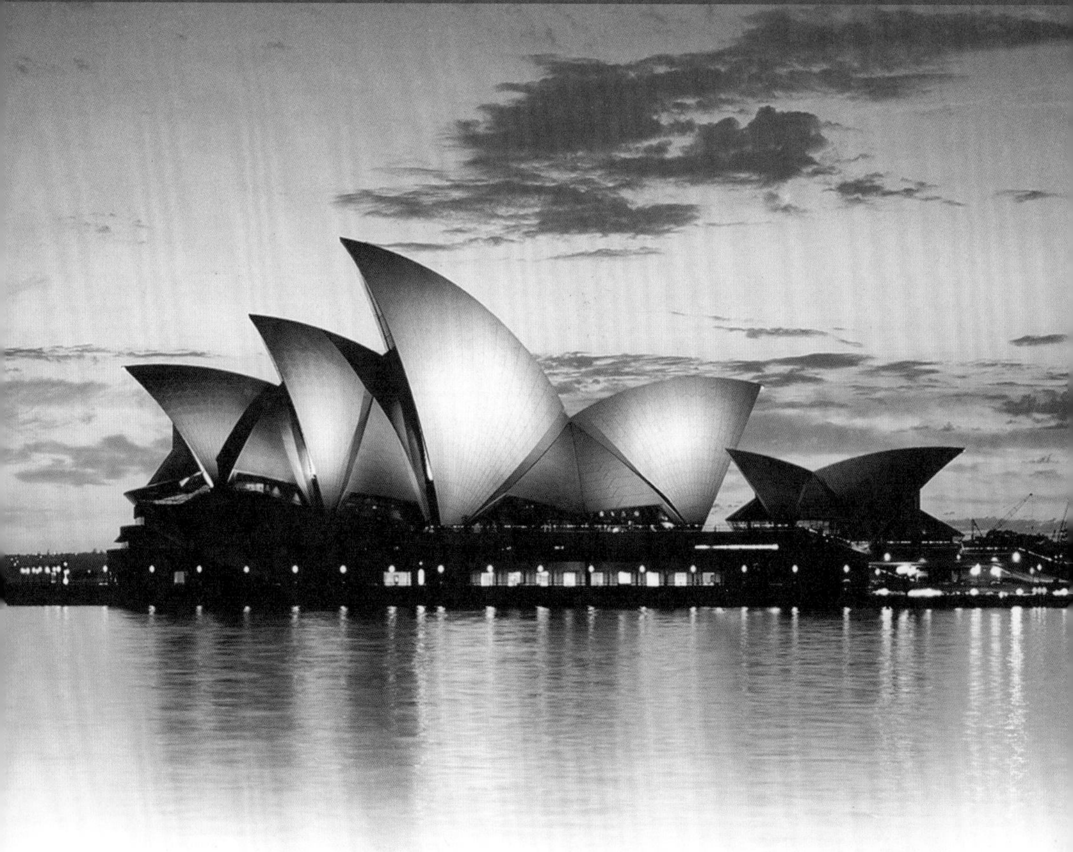

Sydney Opera House

Sydney, Australia

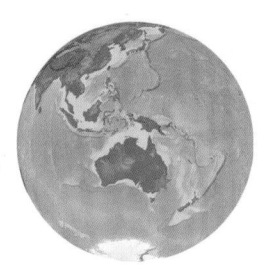

This beautiful theater opened in 1973—about 40 years ago. It sits on a point out in Sydney Harbour in Australia. It was designed by Jørn Utzon to look like nesting shells.

Delicate Arch

Arches National Park, Moab, Utah

This sandstone rock arch overlooks a desert valley. Wind and water loosened the sandy rock to form a "window."

The Matterhorn

Border of Italy and Switzerland

This looks like a pyramid, but it is a mountain in the Alps. Mountaineers have climbed this 14,693-foot rock—but not many!

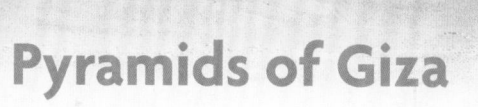

Pyramids of Giza

Near Cairo, Egypt

These pyramids were built 4,500 years ago as royal tombs for Egyptian rulers. The Great Pyramid was made with two million stone blocks.

Gateway Arch

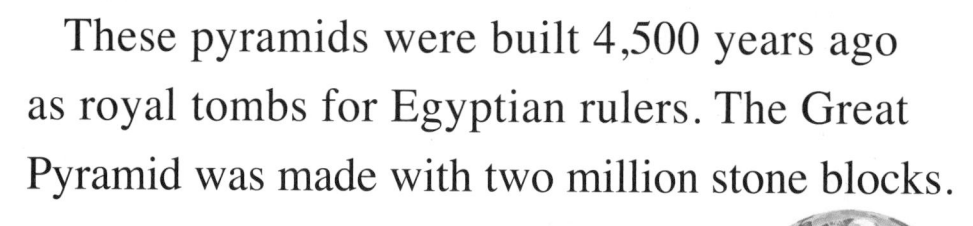

St. Louis, Missouri

At 630 feet, this arch is the tallest monument in the United States. It was made with concrete and steel. It celebrates the city of St. Louis as the "Gateway to the West."

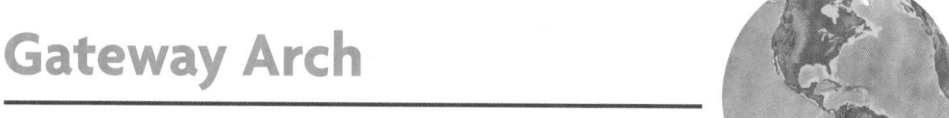

Statue of Liberty

Liberty Island, New York Harbor, NY

This statue was a gift from France to the United States in 1886. It is a statue of Libertas, the Roman goddess of freedom. She is made of pure copper over a steel framework. She stands 151 feet tall atop a 154-foot base.

Mount Rushmore

Near Rapid City, South Dakota

How did Gutzon Borglum carve these four 60-foot faces into a granite mountain? With carefully placed dynamite! The sculpture honors four American presidents: George Washington, Thomas Jefferson, Theodore Roosevelt, and Abraham Lincoln.

Grand Canyon

Northern Arizona

The Colorado River carved this deep canyon. All the colorful layers of rock are exposed, making this a grand sight. At its widest part, the canyon is 18 miles across. At its deepest part, it plunges more than a mile down. Now, that's a canyon!

Niagara Falls

New York State and Canada

Niagara Falls is a set of huge waterfalls on the Niagara River. The most famous are Horseshoe Falls, located on the Canadian side. The water plummets with a thunderous roar and sends up a beautiful mist filled with rainbows.

Mount Kilimanjaro

Tanzania

The Equator runs through some of the hottest places on Earth. Yet right near the Equator are the snow-capped peaks of Mount Kilimanjaro. Its summit is the highest point in Africa—19,340 feet up! "Kilimanjaro" is a Masai word meaning "Large Rock."

The Great Enclosure

Zimbabwe

Some of the walls of this 700-year-old fortress are 20 feet thick. Some walls are 40 feet high! The granite stones fit tightly together with no cement or mortar. How did people do that? And who built it? No one knows for sure.

Great Sphinx of Giza

Near Cairo, Egypt

Near the Pyramids of Giza rests this 4,500-year-old statue. It is 65 feet tall and 241 feet long! It has the head of a man and the body of a lion. Whose face is it? That is the riddle of the Sphinx!

Machu Picchu

Near Cusco, Peru

   More than a mile up in the mountains of Peru lie the ruins of an ancient Incan city—Machu Picchu. It was built around 1450 A.D. The buildings were all made with polished stone blocks without mortar. It's a *l-o-n-g* walk up to see this place!

Angel Falls

Canaima National Park, Venezuela

Angel Falls is the world's highest free-falling waterfall. It plunges 3,212 feet from the top of a flat-topped mountain in Venezuela. The drop is so long, that before the water reaches the bottom, it is blown by strong winds and becomes a lovely mist.

Stonehenge

Near Salisbury, England

Out in an English field stand huge stones—some capped with other stones—formed in a circle. They are ancient—dating to 4,000 years ago! Who erected these 25-ton stones? And why? Archeologists are not sure. What do you think Stonehenge was used for?

Saint Basil's Cathedral

Red Square, Moscow, Russia

Saint Basil's Cathedral was ordered built by Ivan the Terrible and was completed in 1560 A.D. Originally it was painted white with gold "onion" domes. In 1860, the cathedral was repainted with colorful designs. Wouldn't that be a fun art project?

Eiffel Tower

Paris, France

The Eiffel Tower was designed by Gustave Eiffel and built out of iron in 1889 by 300 steel workers. It stands almost 1,000 feet high and was the world's tallest building until 1930. The paint that covers it weighs 40 tons!

Leaning Tower of Pisa

Pisa, Italy

Ever since building began in 1173 A.D. on the bell tower of the Cathedral of Pisa, the tower has leaned. Over the next 200 years, builders tried to correct for the angle. Engineers still work on it today to keep it from falling. The tower stands 186 feet—on its *higher* side.

Petra

Jordan

This 2,000-year-old city was carved out of stone from the slopes of Mount Hor. The many temples and buildings were chiseled by hand! It was lost for centuries—and was rediscovered in 1812. "Petra" means "rock" in Greek. It is believed that at one time 25,000 people lived in Petra.

Ancient Babylon

Iraq

The ruins of Ancient Babylon are in an area once called Mesopotamia. The city may date to 2300 B.C. From 1770–1670 B.C., it was the largest city in the world. The Hanging Gardens of Babylon are listed as one of the Seven Wonders of the Ancient World.

Taj Mahal

Agra, India

When Emperor Shah Jahan's favorite wife died in childbirth, he was grief-stricken. He had a huge tomb built for her, which was finished in 1648. It is made of white marble and is inlaid with gemstones from around the world. 1,000 elephants were used to transport the building materials.

Itsukushima Torii

Off the island of Itsukushima, Japan

At high tide, this beautiful wooden torii (gate) appears to float in the water. It was built in 1875 to welcome the spirits of the dead to the Shinto Shrine that sits on the island. At low tide, visitors can walk up to the 52-foot-high gate. They place coins in the cracks of the legs and make wishes.

Great Wall of China

Northern China

    This earthen, wooden, stone, and brick wall is the world's longest man-made structure—4,160 miles long! It was built by millions of workers starting around 500 B.C. to protect the northern borders of the Chinese Empire. It took about 1,000 years to build!

Angkor Wat

Angkor, Cambodia

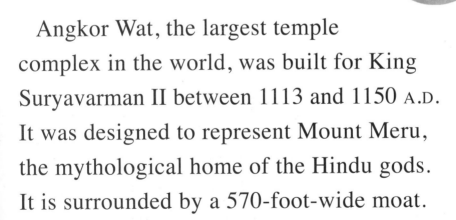

Angkor Wat, the largest temple
complex in the world, was built for King
Suryavarman II between 1113 and 1150 A.D.
It was designed to represent Mount Meru,
the mythological home of the Hindu gods.
It is surrounded by a 570-foot-wide moat.

Great Barrier Reef

Australia

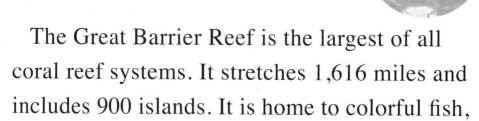

The Great Barrier Reef is the largest of all coral reef systems. It stretches 1,616 miles and includes 900 islands. It is home to colorful fish, sea anemones, starfish, sea turtles, sea snakes, crocodiles, dolphins, sharks, and whales. Of all the world's special places, this is one of its most beautiful landmarks.